T0129668

A DOVE
Released

Poetry and Praise

PATRICIA NIEMANN

WESTBOW
PRESS®
A DIVISION OF THOMAS NELSON
& ZONDERVAN

WestBow Press books may be ordered through
booksellers or by contacting:

WestBow Press
A Division of Thomas Nelson & Zondervan
1663 Liberty Drive
Bloomington, IN 47403
www.westbowpress.com
844-714-3454

Scripture quotations are taken from The Holy Bible, New
International Version®, NIV® Copyright © 1973, 1978, 1984, 2011
by Biblica, Inc.® Used by permission. All rights reserved worldwide.

ISBN: 978-1-6642-9364-9 (sc)
ISBN: 978-1-6642-9363-2 (e)

Library of Congress Control Number: 2023903530

Print information available on the last page.

WestBow Press rev. date: 03/20/2023

Contents

A Dove Released

So is my word that goes forth from my mouth: It will not
return to me empty, but will accomplish what I desire
and achieve the purpose for which I sent it.
—*Isaiah 55:11*

In dark stillness, deep calls to deep.[1]
Before me a nocturnal quest.
Roaming words to capture and tame.
Tonight I must let go of sleep.

Wrestling, revising, changing lines.
Words to untangle and refine.
At last a poem comes to life
As through the curtain daybreak shines.

Adieu to the unsettled night.
With day comes prose and praise entwined.
Receive from me what first You gave.
An offering is poised for flight.

Poem inspired by a King
Released into the open sky.
A soaring, swooping, gliding dove
With scripture on its pure-white wings.

---

[1] Psalm 42:7

The Wood-Plank Swing

For since the creation of the world God's invisible
qualities—his eternal power and divine nature—have
been clearly seen, being understood from what has
been made, so that men are without excuse.
—Romans 1:20

Beneath the swing hard dusty ground,
But on this wood plank I'm heaven-bound.
Two cords of rope I hold on tight,
Then back and forth with all my might.
Fluttering hem and trailing hair,
Kick off my sandals in the air.
Then by chance lean back and see
A sprawling oak-leaf canopy,
Ten thousand leaves waving to me.
Who choreographed this scene
Of steady blue and swaying green?
One Creator over all
Delights to show, display, enthrall.
The heart sings out; the soul takes flight.
Shine down on me, celestial light.
And suddenly, to break the spell,
The *clang!* of Grannie's dinner bell.
Slowly I descend once more.
Grannie's at the kitchen door.
My dusty feet, Grannie's chagrin.
"Child, wash your hands and wipe your chin."

Once again the clouds roll in,
Clutter, busyness, and din.
But in Grannie's yard there stood that day
A towering arbor vitae.
And I will never be the same.
The Book of Life safeguards my name.

The Trellis

Those who are victorious will inherit all this, and I
will be their God and they will be my children.
—*Revelation 21:7*

A lattice to support the vines
Crisscrossed and painted white.
As roses cleave and intertwine,
Their faces turned toward the sun,
They beckon you, "Come, rest a while,"
As dusk gives way to night.

And thus your day came to a close,
Rocking in your oak-wood chair.
Scented air, what sweet repose.
Hands resting on varnished wood
Lift only to tuck in place
A stray lock of winter hair.

This is how I remember you.
Did you often think of me?
Grandma, if you only knew.
Blind was I for so long.
But light has made a heart to bloom,
And now at last I see.

Grandma, did you often pray
As you watched the fall of night
That somehow there would come a day,
By grace, at the appointed time,
When the Word like a trellis
Would lift and turn me toward the light?

Blood-related not once but twice.
Members of a royal line
Thanks be to a sacrifice.
Himself supported by a frame.
Thorns and thistles, red on wood.
This gift is yours and mine.

I've ceased to ramble, ceased to roam.
As they gather from west to east,
Don't worry, Grandma, I'll be home.
At the banquet, I'll be there.
Grafted into the family,
We'll take our places at the feast.

The Gentleness of Your Hands

Honor her for all that her hands have done,
and let her works bring her praise at the city gate.
—*Proverbs 31:31*

Thank you, Mom, for the gentleness of your hands
That applied a brush to white paper and turned it from bleak to charming
With watercolor images like a scarecrow surrounded by pumpkins
And a farm girl and her dog walking to school.
And skating on a frozen pond, children with rosy cheeks and long, fluttering scarves.
Your gentle hands carefully placed the needle on a vinyl disc.
And when you looked at us, your brown eyes sparkled.
You smiled and announced, "This is the Scottish Fantasy."
Our living room with its yellow-and-gold shag carpet
Became a concert hall.
Not the kind where children must sit still.
In our concert hall, we danced and waved our arms like we were conducting
This work by Max Bruch for orchestra and solo violin.
The music surrounded us like the highlands of Scotland.
Your gentle hands turned for us the pages of library books,
Full-page glossy photos of nature and national parks,
Subjects that inspire artists.
You showed us their paintings.
You taught us to notice form and color.
And you especially loved the paintings of Vincent van Gogh.
His birds fly over yellow-and-gold wheat fields.
His sunflowers remind me of you.

Autumn gold, white winter lace, the tender green of spring and summer's shady grove,
You watched the treetops from your Georgia mountain home.
From your artist's table you painted watercolor greeting cards
To send to grandchildren living far away.
With gentle hands perhaps you paused to scratch Scherzo behind the ears
As he lounged by your feet.
Always listening to music, your favorite song was "Somewhere over the Rainbow,"
A song about the home we yearn for.
You're there now, Mom. Home with your Lord and Savior.
We remember the gentleness of your hands.

The Memory of a Rose

Our days ... quickly pass, and we fly away.
—*Psalm 90:10*

A life in bloom with us can't stay.
Gently the petals fall away
Year by year and day by day.
Why and how long no one knows,
But we'll remember at the close
How lovely was the life, the rose.

My Daughter, My Prayer

Jesus said, "Let the little children come to me."
—*Matthew 19:14*

Dear heavenly Father,
My daughter came in late spring.
As if to welcome her, the garden bloomed,
Its flowers open to the sun above.
I remember little else.
I was in another place
Somewhere between earth and paradise.
I must have caught a glimpse of heaven
When I gazed into my newborn's eyes.
I did nothing to deserve this gift.
I have nothing to offer in return
Except to whisper a prayer of thanks.
For of such a miracle I can barely speak.
In silent awe I hold my child,
Of whom an angel spoke to me
In a dream before her birth.
Father, Your love rains down on us.
Give me wisdom, give me strength.
Help me raise my child.
Together we'll walk in Your light.
Until the day she releases me,
When she lets go of my hand
To follow her own path of dreams.
You know the plans You have for her.
In truth she belongs to You.

Though I may cry a little,
I know Your love will keep her
All the days of her life.
Give her Your blessings, Father.
In Jesus's name I pray.
Amen.

The Dogwood Tree
(Outside Your Window)

To everything there is a season, and a time
to every purpose under heaven ...
—*Ecclesiastes 3*

Each member of the snow quartet
Departs for its solo descent.
What was a splendid wedding gown
Is now a carpet on the ground,
Edges curled and turning brown.
But do not fret; no need for grief.
Behold the season of the leaf.
Then blushing in the autumn air,
Disrobed in winter, branches bare.
Seasons melt into each other.
One today and then another.
For you perhaps they moved too slow.
Aspiring, agile, and aglow
While you gazed through the windowpane,
Your mind boarded the future train
And foresaw peaks and alpine trails,
Sky-top towns and wildflower dales.
But blossom time is not for long.
Before I knew it, you were gone.
The dogwood with its branches high
Reminds me birds are meant to fly.
As now my eyes look through the pane,
Blossoms depart but leaves remain.
Love to receive and love to give.
'Tis in this moment that I live.

A Visit, A Bouquet

A time to scatter stones and a time to gather them.
—*Ecclesiastes* 3:5

Come home in springtime
When Demeter opens wide her arms.
That's how I'd welcome you.
Can the give and take that is your life
Release you for a while?
Can what's been widely scattered
Be for a short time gathered?
A forsythia bush near the wood
Throws off wintertime constraints.
With riotous yellow blooms
Growing in all directions.
I've collected some cuttings
And placed them in a mason jar
For your room (though I know they won't last long)
Hoping that you'll visit soon.
We'll gather like cut flowers,
Our visit an arranged bouquet.
If not in spring, then summer,
Wintertime, or fall.
It matters not how brief.
The seasons visit once a year.
Just come home for a spell,
Any time at all.

Flamingo Flowers

Whatever is lovely, whatever is admirable- if anything is
excellent or praiseworthy- think about such things.
—Philippians 4:8

You tall dahlias that tower
On lanky, spindly stems
Like birds balanced on one thin leg.
If you could talk, you'd surely squawk.
Let's call you "flamingo flower."
Your pink-puff tops with petals
Like tiny tufted plumes.
Some blooms look down toward the ground.
Others toward the sky.
Heads that turn every which way
With a yellow center eye.
Rosy like the blush of dawn.
Blithe and merry, joyful, jocund
Flamingos standing on my lawn.

At the Place of Awe

Be exalted, O God, above the heavens; let
your glory be over all the earth.
—Psalm 57:5

Shrouded in white milky mist,
Cool and damp the upturned face
Watching the cascade thunder down,
Standing at the plunge pool base.
From this viewpoint, look way up high.
As though spilling out of clouds,
A deluge plummets from the sky.
Speechless before the waterfall.
Experience knows naught of words,
Silence at the place of awe.
A gentler awe like drops of dew
Desires only to endear
When newborn eyes gaze up at you.
At the touch of rose-petal skin,
A deluge of the heartfelt kind
Overflows from deep within.
Forever changed by one so small,
Experience knows naught of words,
Silence at the place of awe.
Murky waters now run clear.
The Creator and source of awe
Seeks to gather, to draw us near.
The mighty takes the form of meek
To close the gap widened by fear.
Humbling Himself by human birth.
Hearts unfold, Him to receive
When heaven reaches down to earth.

Slumber

He is before all things, and in him all things hold together.
—Colossians 1:17

The waters rise; the waters fall.
I see the ocean breathing.
A murmur, a soft rhythmic snore.
I hear the ocean sleeping.
Until the moon shines overhead,
Water lapping, low tide drifting,
Shifting on a sandbar bed.
He who numbers each grain of sand,
Who never sleeps but watch He keeps
Cups the ocean in His hands.

The Mariner and the Moon

Where can I go from your Spirit? Where can I flee from your presence? If I go up to the heavens, you are there; if I make my bed in the depths, you are there. If I rise on the wings of the dawn, if I settle on the far side of the sea, even there your hand will guide me, your right hand will hold me fast.
—*Psalm 139:7-10*

Was there a time before the moon?

A glowing pearl in a velvet sky.
A sentinel to gaze upon.
Nightly near, always nigh.
Sign of a presence felt yet unseen.
Who knit the question deep and sound
In the mariner's inmost being?

The sea's morning calm and caress
Beneath a sunlit sheen.
By evening terror and duress.
Watery hands toss and torment,
Relentless in their roughhouse play,
Leave the mariner tired, spent.

Delivered on a foreign shore
Whose town welcomes the sojourner,
The mariner is safe once more.
Courage renewed and mended sail,
The mariner must bid farewell
Ahead of storm, ahead of gale.

At midnight silver moonbeams rest
On weathered oak and rusting hinge,
Casting light on an old sea chest.
When this sailboat was in repair,
A kind, wizened fisher of men
Discreetly must have placed it there.

Inside the box the ancient chart.
A map to steer the course of life
Reveals a Father's loving heart.
The mariner reads undeterred
And marvels when a page proclaims,
"In the beginning was the Word." [2]

The Word before land, sea, or sky.
A revelation parts the clouds.
This doubting mariner was I.
For now the night shines like the day.
The veil of early morning haze.
Truth, like the sun, has burned away.

Back to that port across the sea.
Breath of God, fill soul and sail.
Be swift my vessel, hard-a-lee.
Out of the irons, now I'm free
And eager to return again
To thank the one who thought of me.

Listen, you waves and sapphire star,
All suspended celestial spheres,
To you the planets near and far
I sing a joyful tune.
A new song in my mouth declares,
There was a time before the moon.

---

2 John 1:1

Night Sky

A message written in the sky,
"Great and unequaled am I."
In glittering nighttime displays,
A reminder to those who gaze.
"Glory to God!" the stars proclaim.
He calls them forth, each one by name.[3]
And so we are without excuse.
Lights abounding and profuse.
A firmament that does not end,
Too vast for minds to comprehend.
But He meets us where we are.
God in the flesh; the Morning Star.
Follow the light and Him we'll find.
Clothed in His light we'll brightly shine.

---

[3] Isaiah 40:26

Seabirds of Half Moon Bay

Look at the birds of the air; they do not sow or reap
or store away in barns, and yet your heavenly Father
feeds them. Are you not more valuable than they?
—*Matthew 6:26*

Silver swells, white frothy foam,
And sky of pearly gray.
Seabirds circling over cliffs.
Craggy bluffs that thwart the tide.
Though eroded they remain
Sentries of Half Moon Bay.

Scattered the fragmented shells
Pieces of sapphire blue.
Mosaics pressed into wet sand,
Tumbled, crushed in gritty surf.
Still they retain the luster
Of iridescent hue.

Caught between jagged edges,
A tool for lift and flight.
And for me a souvenir
Of today's beach and bluff hike.
A feather, white like a cloud
And tipped with blackest night.

A fallen plume, no great loss
For divers of the sky.
No rough waves do they battle.
Sea gulls, terns, and cormorants
Watch the drama down below
From places way up high.

When troubles surge like a wave,
I can't take to the air.
Still, my soul is free to glide.
He who overcame the world
And keeps my feet from stumbling
Will all my burdens bear.

A Change of Heart

Forget the former things; do not dwell on the
past. See, I am doing a new thing!
—Isaiah 43:18

A rainbow is a change of heart;
A new direction on the chart.
Turn away and turn toward.
Forgive the past and move forward.
Through the clouds, these prisms shine
When light and water drops combine.
A sign His wrath has moved away
Like storm clouds on a tempest day.
Water in the form of rain
Once filled the earth from peak to plain.
Every form of life submerged.
Floods to cleanse, expel, and purge
The disobedience and sin
And idolatries therein.
But wrath is not the final end
For a heart that seeks to mend.
To restore, replenish, renew
The ark's creatures two by two.
Noah and his descendants,
He blessed their lives as recompense.
And promised to never again
Destroy the earth by flood, amen.
The covenant sealed with His mark—
The colors of the rainbow arc.

Gratitude

Give thanks in all circumstances; for this is
God's will for you in Christ Jesus.
—1 Thessalonians 5:18

The origin of discontent,
A tendency, a human bent.
When paradise did not suffice,
The crafty serpent's own device.
But Satan has not fully won.
Discontent can be overcome.
This is what gratitude can do,
Itself a godly point of view.
Gratitude, like bread of heaven.
White manna without leaven.
Spiritual food for the soul,
To give thanks, and Him, extol.

On the Sandbar
(Where I Meet God)

Be still and know that I am God; I will be exalted
among the nations, I will be exalted in the earth.
—Psalm 46:10

A castle of the golden age
To shelter Sir Knight and his page.
With portcullis and parapet
And looming tower silhouette.
A drawbridge hewn of ancient oak
Across a deep-dredged circle moat.
Thickness of wall and fortified
Until the enemy, the tide.
With foamy stretch and lazy yawn,
A masterwork of sand soon gone.
Gone his crimson waving banner.
The feisty lord of the manor
Amidst flotsam and debris,
Has scuttled back into the sea.
Away the shovel and the pail.
Silence the storm, the inward gale.
Peace and solitude to find.
Leave the sand and shore behind.
Feet on the sandbar, water calm,
Steady in an open palm.
Diamond, raindrop, glassy sea,
The color of eternity.

The abundance You turn to me
Reminds me of my destiny.
Your Father's manse beyond the sky,
A place for me; a room have I.
And this Your promise You will keep
When I awaken from the sleep.

Thoughts on Cervantes's
Don Quijote de la Mancha

For where your treasure is, there your heart will be also.
—Matthew 6:21

His lady fair he's never kissed.
Dulcinea, real as vapor,
As elusive as the dawn,
Beautiful as mist.
No knights on horseback will he find
Except in dusty corners,
Rooms of forgotten clutter,
The cobwebs of his mind.
Centuries of neglect and rust,
He's put on ancestral armor
And saddled up the stable nag.
Resolved, this knight errant must
Free the oppressed, right the wrongs,
And rid the land of evil.
To be the glorious hero
Of legends, poems, and songs.
Vigil by night, battle by day.
Don Quijote, gallant and brave.
While Sancho, his rustic squire,
Seeks from his master steady pay.
A comic pair as they set out.
The master, tall and gaunt
With makeshift helmet, lance, and shield.
His squire on a donkey,
Sancho short and stout.

Misadventures around each bend.
The master, thrown off his horse
While charging after windmills.
Faithful Sancho dusts him off
And sets him back on course.
Something of worth, value and real,
Forged on the dirt roads of Castile
That moths and rust could not destroy
Nor thieves conspire to steal.
Days turn to months and still they ride.
An alliance, a treasure,
Two halves of a smooth gold coin
When vision and reality
Go traveling side by side.
Ride on, ride on noble friends.
Someday the true Knight will return
To bring justice to all the earth.
A new dawn when the old world ends.

Kalends

I saw the Holy City, the new Jerusalem, coming down out of heaven
from God, prepared as a bride beautifully dressed for her husband.
—*Revelation 21:2*

December thirty and one,
Another lap around the sun.
How predictable you are.
Tethered to a fiery star.
With your movement for a base,
Events, our lives are held in place.
We track the days and count them all
Like tallies on a prison wall.
On New Year's Day, how very strange
To celebrate no real change.
The old order once passed away
Will be the longed-for freedom day.
A new heaven; a new earth.
Rejuvenation and rebirth.
Eden cried after the Fall.
But You've come to redeem us all.
And when at last You come again,
The timeline will have reached its end.
Then Your city, we shall behold.
Sapphire, emerald, streets of gold.
Living waters from Your well.
God shall among His people dwell.

The Gleam of Hope

"At that time I will gather you; at that time I will bring you home. I will give you honor and praise among all the peoples of the earth when I restore your fortunes before your very eyes," says the Lord.
—*Zephaniah 3:20*

Days of youth, it would suffice
To admit I lost them twice.
The first time when they ceased to be;
The second from my memory.
Increasingly these take their place:
A knowing heart, a wizened face.
Alas! Where can one find reprieve
From the constant sifting sieve?
What was valued turns to dross.
If time would cease, so would loss.
Hope the gleaming gold remains
To free from bondage, break the chains.
For what was lost You will restore.
Paradise forevermore.

Esteemed Dandelion

Every good and perfect gift is from above, coming
down from the Father of the heavenly lights.
—James 1:17

In August, overlooked, ignored,
Trampled under flip-flop feet.
Life vests and oars land on your head.
Covered by the picnic spread.
Enduring sun and summer heat.
But come November you're adored.

Yellow dab on a dreary day.
I'd hold you up to any mum.
Those who stroll by would agree,
You're the peak of tenacity.
This time of year, you're not outdone.
Bright button on a coat of gray.

I'll see you in the aftermath
When cutting winds and ice storms pass.
The lake a mirror of the clouds.
Calm before the summer crowds.
Thanks be to God above, steadfast
For placing hope along my path.

Je Crois (I Believe)

For there is one God and one mediator between
God and mankind, the man Christ Jesus.
—1 Timothy 2:5

I place my hand with fingers spread
Against gritty, granular stone.
This is the moment I need to live, a pivot
When the gap closes between me and ancient Rome.
I traveled forward to go back in time.
Far below I see a yellow speck, a kayak
Slowly emerge from a colossal shadow that darkens
The Gardon River.
The sentry, the Pont du Gard, with its towering arches
Once channeled enough water
To fill the fountains, public baths, and houses of Roman citizens.
An insatiable thirst.
I've touched its hand, and now I believe in ancient Rome.
And I believe in a monument made of wood, not stone.
This and others stood on the Roman landscape
With no name and not meant to mark power and might,
But rather, criminal shame.
On one of these, the savior died and on the third day, rose again.
Jesus, who came to earth at the time of the Roman cross,
The appointed time,
To be a bridge between us and God.
Himself the living water that satisfies our thirst.
Je crois, la croix, I believe.

Ode to a Roman Road

Teach me your way, Lord; lead me in a straight path.
—*Psalm 27:11*

Like a spoke that joins a hub,
Straight is this road to Rome.
No hill will it circumvent; no peak obstructs its view.
This road tunnels through mountain base.
Boulders removed to clear its path
Proclaim the might of Rome.
From rock-fed trench to cement bond then paved with fitted stone.
The work of slaves, of bloodied hands.
This fortress lying in its bed,
Locks down the conquered lands.
Marching armies tread this road, legions of marionettes.
Veni, vidi, vici, scripted
Before time began.
Caesar and his famous line,
Part of a master plan.
And because the setting drives the plot,
This Roman road serves well.
The Empire was no accident.
No random rise and fall.
A road used by Julius Caesar
Would likewise be used by Paul.
A paved road used to spread the Word
Across continents and sea.
A network to conquer and enslave
Now sets the captive free.
The ancient wheel dissolved by rust.

Beneath one's feet, the empire's dust.
But sojourners still walk this road.
Timeworn guideposts line its path
And fountains to refresh.
Now and then, a pasture green
Where a weary soul finds rest.
Lord keep me on this road to home.
Prone am I to stray.
Keep my focus on the cross.
Lord show me the way.

Thoughts on Homer's The Odyssey

*What is mankind that you are mindful of them,
human beings that you care for them?*
—Psalm 8:4

Release this mortal to the sea.
Goddess Calypso, set him free.
His heart remembers her who waits.
His mind's eye sees her at the gates.
This hero of a foreign war
Yearns for his homeland all the more.

Perilous, the journey home.
Dark waters lead to worlds unknown.
Hold fast, Odysseus, be strong.
All fates to the god Zeus belong.
Pray as you face adversity
For his protection on the sea.
Lotus, a snare for your defeat.
Woe to you if this you eat.
With guile and cunning you defy
And blind the giant's only eye.
Tormented by a vengeful hand.
Poseidon, shaker of the land.
Goddess Circe delayed your quest.
Seduced by her, weakened, obsessed.

The gods delight to toy with him.
They help or hinder at their whim.
There is the one God who pursues
While others distract and confuse.
The Author and the Hero one,
God the father and His Son
Who came to earth with us to dwell.
God in the flesh, Emmanuel.
The lost who drift and further roam,
He gave His life to bring them home.
His heart's desire at all cost
Since the day of paradise lost.
Across mountains, over the sea,
Through the ages a living tree.
Alpha, omega steadfast
The one true epic, first and last.

The Island of If Only

Listen, my sons, to a father's instruction; pay
attention and gain understanding.
—*Proverbs 4:1*

"Father!"
The last word of a cherished youth.
A plea for help, a desperate cry
Of one who tried to reach the sun.
Wings held with wax that came undone,
Melted and in disarray,
Falling from the sky.
"Icarus, where are you?"
Too late to save and no reply.
Feathers floating on the sea.
And once again, captivity.
Daedalus, a prisoner,
Solitary and lonely,
Exiled to an inward isle,
The island of If Only …

If only he would have listened
And followed my path of flight.
A plan so fraught with danger.
If only I'd thought twice.
Escape from the island of Crete
At far too great a price.

Youth with fire in your eyes,
Before you take off to the skies,
Live long and take heed to the wise.
Fly not too high and not too low
But somewhere in the midrange go.
And keep from the island of pain,
The one who loves you so.

The Sunday School Class

Train up a child in the way he should go: and
when he is old, he will not depart from it.
—Proverbs 22:6

Starting at the column base,
An upward move, a tight embrace.
Should there be a wayward vine,
Redirect it on the twine.
In support of one another,
Let them wrap around each other.
In their centers yellow, bright
Blue morning glories greet the light.
Eager and wanting to know
What to follow, where to go.
Give them access to a string
On which to travel as they cling.
Raising them to heights utmost,
The steadfast alabaster post.

Thoughts I Could Not Tell

In the same way, let your light shine before others that they
may see your good deeds and glorify your Father in Heaven.
—*Matthew 5:16*

To my students:

Every morning we stood
For the Pledge of Allegiance.
Then a moment of silence.
In that space I would
Pray for Him to rule and reign
Over our classroom
As I taught you the language of
The Americas and Spain.
I tried always to see you
As "fearfully and wonderfully made,"[4]
Even on difficult days,
But this you never knew.
I tried to be a light
Through acts of kindness and compassion,
(Such is needed in public school)
Hoping it would shine through in spite
Of bells, noisy halls, and bog.
Making clear,
Showing the way
Out of confusion and fog.

---

[4] Psalm 139:14

The yearbooks, I was pleased to sign,
Writing "*Dios te bendiga.*"
Trusting that He would bless you
With wisdom divine.

His path to truth.
To question and wrestle,
A yearning to know
While still in your youth.
Keep sifting through the dross,
Keep searching.
The truth is real and everlasting,
Waiting for you at the foot of the cross.
This is my final farewell.
Goodbye, my students, and God bless.
These are my parting thoughts to you.
The ones I could not tell.

Departure

His master replied, "Well done, good and faithful servant!"
—*Matthew 25:23*

Asleep beneath your wintry cap
When frost and crystal cling.
A frilly floral bonnet
Awakening in spring.
And still loyal to the fold,
Summer, your shady parasol.
Autumn, your crown of gold.
Gently I land in a stream.
Here ends my seasons' story.
Slowly I depart from you,
Adrift in gilded glory.
When winter comes, remember me.
Come spring, let go of sorrow.
Carry on tall, stalwart tree,
Tomorrow and tomorrow.

The Daisy Field (Vita Brevis)

All people are like grass, and all their glory is like the
flowers of the field; the grass withers and the flowers
fall, but the word of the Lord endures forever.
—Isaiah 40:6-8

In each center, a tiny sun.
White petals for its rays.
Plucking daisies one by one,
Enough for two bouquets.

Endless daisies greet the morn.
A bedspread on the land.
Barefoot on my path to home,
A treasure in each hand.

From meadow to water-filled jar,
And still I have some space
To add long-stemmed goldenrod
And roadside Queen Anne's lace.

Flowers gathered and arranged
Artfully and finessed.
Languid hours still remain
For contentment and rest.

The sun's departing masterpiece
Across a canvas sky.
Rosy orange takes its bow.
Sprite dancers wilt and die.

The memory of that daisy field,
A distant bird in flight.
Swiftly flies the day on wings
And pending is the night.

All things created take their leave,
But You alone remain.
Stay with me as shadows fall.
Your story tell again.

The prince who ransomed his beloved.
You are the prince made known.
Your book, a treasure in my hands.
Your book, my path to home.

Scenes from a Train

In my flesh shall I see God.
—Job 19:26

A gray stone chapel's open doors
With magnolia to one side.
The perfect frame when they appear,
The bridegroom and his bride.
Oh the gladness of that day,
The tree a pink-and-white bouquet.
Watercolor leaves of green,
The first-time blush of gentle spring,
Deepens to a summer scene.

A mother's push and she takes flight
Seated on a wood plank swing.
Secured with rope and knotted tight
Around the strong arm of a tree.
She's leaning back and gaining height.
Beneath the oak leaf canopy.
In me a stir, a quiet swell.
Her laughter and that daisy dress
I remember well.

On to the next scene, turn the page.
She's packed her bags and leaving home.
The child has grown and come of age.
Buried words parents can't speak.
A moment overshadows years.
A tear runs down a ruddy cheek.
The sympathetic dogwood tree

Slowly drops its crimson leaf.
The season of letting go.

Now through the window, frost and snow.
A couple walking down the lane,
One foot placed and then the next.
They pause and turn to watch the train.
A little stooped, a little bent,
Like pine boughs under heavy snow.
The weight of years together spent.
His arm around her pulls her close,
Attached to what is loved and known.
As pine cone clings to pine bough home.
How sad to think of him alone.

How like a curtain falls the night.
No baggage did I bring on board.
The forgiven travel light.
Nor did I buy a ticket.
I was told I need not pay,
That someone else had paid the cost
Of this passage one-way.
I notice a white blanket
On the seat next to me.
Did the conductor leave it there
When I was lost in reverie?
I'll stretch out on this empty seat
And close my eyes to the moonlight.
This covering to keep me safe
Is all the warmth I need tonight.

At dawn as I step off the train,
His hands reach out to steady me,
To keep my feet from stumbling.
And in the center of each palm,
A scar where the nail used to be.

In every season, He was there.
All the days ordained for me
In His keeping, in His care.

Kingdom gates flung open wide.
Next to them the living tree.
Beyond this His Father's mansion
Where He's prepared a place for me.
At once I'm rich beyond compare.
Resplendent in His righteousness,
This new garment that I wear.
His victory and now mine won.
Let eternity begin.
Home everlasting with the Son.

Stepping Stones

All the days ordained for me were written in your
book before one of them came to be.
—Psalm 139:16

"You're all grown up."
"I am."

"You're going to college."
"I am."

"You're getting married."
"You're a first-time parent."
"You're an empty nester."

"I am."
"I am."
"I am."

"You're saved!"
"*I am!*"

"You're retiring."
"I am."

"You're getting old."
"I am."

"You're dying."
"I am."

"You're about to enter
into His glory."
"Amen."
(Final exhale.)

The Choir

Let the heavens rejoice, let the earth be glad; let the sea resound
and all that is in it; let the fields be jubilant, and everything
in them. Then all the trees of the forest will sing for joy.
—Psalm 96:11-12

Steady the expanded wings.
An uplift to catch airstream.
Gliding, the *aves* call and sing.
Silhouettes above the pine.
Their circling updraft, dip and climb,
Follows the soprano line.

The streams continue this theme.
Sparkling, clear, and winding.
Thawed and loosed for their grand scheme.
Below mountain peak and pine,
Runnels to rivers out to sea,
A confluence, an alto line.

Pitched and lobbed in foamy tide,
A buoyant vagabond
Joins the others side by side.
Upward grows the rooted palm.
A tenor line of waving fronds
Performs canticle and psalm.

From whence came their island stage
Of cooled volcanic rock?
A fiery molten rampage
Of unbridled tremolos

Born of earth's deepest register,
Bass note archipelagos.

All creation, find a voice
To magnify your Maker.
Alleluia, sing, rejoice.
You stones that line the narrow road,
Chant hosannas to the Lord.
Sing, all the earth, in choir mode.

Backyard Symphony

Finally, brothers and sisters, whatever is true, whatever
is noble, whatever is right, whatever is pure, whatever
is lovely, whatever is admirable—if anything is excellent
or praiseworthy—think about such things.
—*Philippians 4:8*

Scarlet cardinal, trill your best.
Your *weet-du-weet* resound.
Your solo is my measure rest.
Here in our backyard symphony,
Tweets and chirps abound.

My fingers balanced on the E
Like starlings on a wire.
"La Primavera" by Vivaldi.
His notes mimic the songs of birds
Reaching ever higher.

Triplet sixteenths crossing strings.
Notes metallic and shrill.
My bow arm flapping like a wing
To parody the raucous jays.
Then comes the high-pitched trill.

But I can't trill as fast as you.
What *a divo* you are.
Your entrances always on cue.
How wide is your avian range.
And varied, your repertoire.

(Am I wrong or could it be
With your *canoro* flair
That you delight to mimic me?)
Now in the score, the storm has passed.
Musicians of the air
We return to charming song.
From my window, I can tell
You're moved and stirred to chime along
As bow hair meets taut metal string.
We ensemble well.

Who might be the audience?
Do angels lend an ear?
Waiting for us as we commence
Each note, a praise to God above.
Is it perfect pitch they hear?

Songs I play and those that leap
From branches they intone.
Glad is the company I keep.
One thing solitude teaches me,
Never am I alone.

Of Wood and Wonderment

In him lie hidden all the treasures of wisdom and knowledge.
—*Colossians 2:3*

Spruce and maple together sing
One resonant silken tone.
Transcend the hall; suspend in air.
The playing stops but notes still ring.
No other violin can compare.
And expert eyes cannot ignore
The artistry and allure
Of intricate purfling
And carved scroll curvature.
The Stradivari mystique.
Where does the secret rest?
A quality of sound unmatched,
Three hundred years later science
Puts theories to the test.

An overall consistency
Of increased growth ring density.
Europe's Little Ice Age.
Winter's harsh and extreme cold,
The continent's slow tree growth stage,
Hence full-bodied maple wood.

Conjecture matters little.
Answers sometimes elude.
For now we only know in part.
I must simply conclude,
He tended the dense forest,

His arbor for His plans.
And prevailed over the workshop,
Guiding Stradivari's hands.
Every minute, day and night.
What began as a tree upright
Transformed for His own pleasure,
For His own delight.

No need for argument or strife.
Let mystery and wonder
Be not explained nor understood.
Let them remain as sun and rain
For the soul to flower
Beside the tree of life.

Woven Threads

But the plans of the Lord stand firm forever, the
purposes of his heart through all generations.
—*Psalm 33:11*

Farewell to St. Petersburg.
Newly-married, with violin and aspirations,
She followed her husband to America.
Years later, a luthier in Poland
Applied a final coat and hung the instrument by its scroll to dry.
From this workshop the violin traveled
To the receiving hands of an amateur
Who studies with the Russian violinist
And plays "Dark Eyes" in a Philadelphia railway station.
Somewhere in Pennsylvania, an elderly woman from Eastern Europe
Feels forgotten on her birthday.
A younger woman wearing a suit rushes over, phone in hand.
"Please, would you play that song again?"
She speed dials.
"Mom! I heard this coming up the escalator. Just listen."
I play with plaintive vibrato and tearful slurs.
The final note ends at the tip.
The bow slowly lifts off the string. Silence, and then
"Thank you. Today is my mom's birthday. She was crying on the phone.
Her mother taught her that song."
Threads from all directions came together that day,

Connecting us to each other.
Coincidence, you say?
I think not.
There is a plan in the universe; a heart that beats.
Just listen.

The Cunga Man

This is my commandment, that you love
one another as I have loved you.
—John 15:12

Every sister,
Every brother,
Wake up, rise up.
Love one another.
Feel the rhythm.
Hear the beat.
His drum is calling,
"*Arriba* Philly,
On your feet."
See him busk on Filbert Street.
Shake his hand
When first you meet.
The hands that play
For you by day.
The hands that clasp
At night to pray.
His motto
Remains the same:
Serve the Lord
And bless His name.
Give him a smile
And if you can,
Leave a tip for
The Cunga Man.

The Strength of Humility
(A Tribute to George Washington)

Humility comes before honor.
—*Proverbs 18:12*

Made of woven fabric,
Portable and light.
From within a candle glows.
Hope shines in darkest night.
Alone in makeshift linen rooms
Did he consider at length
As he prayed to Almighty God
That in humility lies strength?
Like Moses doubting himself,
Prepared and equal to the trust.
But meet the king in battle.
Command his troops he must.
Encamped among brawling recruits,
Farmers, trappers, men of the sea
From thirteen distinct colonies.
Quarrels and camp melee.
Washington, a peacemaker then,
The architect of an army,
Of disciplined, fighting men.
Resolve gleaming in their eyes,
Willing to lay down their lives.
Swords to slash and sever ties
To a monarch, distant and cruel
For the cause of liberty.
For freedom and self-rule.

Devoted to their commander
Who will never leave their side.
Deprivation and low moral
When Providence turns the tide.
And when the king concedes defeat,
He puts the sword back in its sheath.
Monarchies watch in disbelief.
Civilian first he then resigns
As commander in chief.
A time for war; a time for peace.
A time to break; a time to bind.
The people's right to rule themselves,
A bold move for humankind.
A president instead of king,
The statesman heeds the call.
A two-term limit self-imposed.
When willfully he steps down,
The whole world stands in awe.
The father of his country
Turns homeward once again
To bucolic Mount Vernon.
A tower among men.

Altitudes

But those who hope in the Lord will renew their strength.
They will soar on wings like eagles; they will run and
not grow weary, they will walk and not be faint.
—*Isaiah 40:31*

The hand that carves the canyon
And curls the crashing wave
Upholds the brown expanded wings.
Pointed plumes designed to soar
Now cease the down-up motion.
Relinquish and rescind.
Floating over mountain peaks.
Gliding on thermal wind.
If I could cast off doubt and fear,
The weights that hold me down,
I'd reach the altitudes with ease.
To be where the eagles dare
And never leave the ground.

The Condor's Wings

He has risen.
—Matthew 28:6

I'm dreaming of a poem
That goes ahead of me.
Words of praise transported
By winds over the sea.
It settles on a condor.
To this raptor it clings.
Skimming over Andean peaks.
Soaring on the wings.

A praise to God in places
Where I can never go.
Canyons, clefts, escarpments,
Mount Aconcagua in snow.
Take it with you, condor,
To heights where you have flown,
To sky-high Machu Picchu
With its perfectly cut stone.

This is my praise, oh condor.
The next sunrise you behold,
Remember that there shines a light
Brighter than Inti's gold.
Stone and mountain sing, rejoice.
All creation find a voice.
Jesus o'er death has won.
Glory to God the Father
And to His risen Son.

Inspiration

All that we have accomplished you have done for us.
—Isaiah 26:12

Words fly like birds across the page.
I, the novice; You, the sage
Whose truth and wisdom you impart
As You direct the mind and heart
And keep them lifted on their course.
Inspiration, You're the source.
Thoughts once weighted by the night,
Freely glide across the white.
Faith awakened and increased.
Forty doves to You released.

Printed in the United States
by Baker & Taylor Publisher Services